Tagged!

Written by Joshua Hatch

Illustrated by Ian Forss

Flying Start
to Literacy®

Contents

Chapter 1

A horrible Sunday

My horrible Sunday started with an alert on my phone. It said, "A video you're tagged in has more than 1,000 likes. See it now!"

I hadn't uploaded any videos. What was happening?

I clicked the link, and up came a video that I recognised immediately by its headline:

"Header Loses Basketball Game."

The video was of my school's basketball team playing against our biggest rivals the previous night. I let out a groan.

******

"Ten, nine, eight," the crowd chanted. I watched the ball leave number 19's hands. He was tall and athletic. He'd been making shots all night. If only he missed this one, then we'd win.

"Seven, six, five . . . " The ball bounced off the rim. I leapt up. If I could grab the ball, I'd be the hero, the victor. I could feel the energy of the crowd. My feet left the ground and my hands reached up. "Four, three, two . . . "

Bonk! I felt the thud against my head, and the ball was up and away. I landed, turned and saw it moving towards the basket.

"One!" the crowd shouted, just as the ball slipped over the rim and through the net. *"BZZZZZZ,"* the buzzer sounded. The other team was jubilant. My teammates looked at me with disdain.

I felt my stomach tighten. The video had been posted two hours earlier and already had 1,054 likes. Someone named Fernando73 had uploaded it and tagged me. That's how my phone knew to send me the alert.

I went back to the page and saw the comments. They certainly didn't make me feel any better.

"Best shot he made all day," said one person.

"Amateur day!" wrote another.

A third comment was just: 👀

But the worst comment was from Fernando73, the person who uploaded the video:

"That goofball is Eric Farnsworth. Good thing the ball hit him on his head, where it wouldn't do any damage."

I didn't know who Fernando73 was, and I didn't want to.

Then I started to wonder. *Have other people posted stuff about me?* I typed my name into the search bar. I hit "enter" and waited for the results to load.

Chapter 2

Baby blog

"I demand answers!" I said, as I came down from my room and saw my family eating breakfast at the table. My brother was pouring syrup on his pancakes and my parents were reading the newspaper.

"And good morning to you, too," my mum replied. "I could use a few answers, too. Like, why didn't you come to breakfast when I called?"

"Sorry, but I just searched my name on the Internet, and do you know what I found?" I asked in a demanding tone.

My parents looked at me. "What?" they asked.

"Baby pictures! And videos! And a blog you wrote when I was a baby and had a rash on my butt!" I didn't mean to be yelling, but I knew I was.

My brother snickered.

"It's humiliating!" I shouted.

"Ah," my mother said. "Why don't you come over here and we'll talk about it."

I walked over and sat down with a loud harrumph.
I wanted her to know that I was upset.

9

"Honey," my mum said in her most soothing voice. "What brought all this on?"

"Someone posted a video of last night's game and my stupid play. Then he posted a comment with my name," I explained, getting emotional. "Now everybody at school will know it's me!"

"Do you think everyone at school doesn't already know?" my brother asked with glee. "I mean really, Eric. There's nobody who's not talking about it."

He was laughing, but I was not.

"What if they see my baby blog? Everyone will make fun of me!"

Then my mum chimed in. "I had forgotten about that baby blog. It was for your grandparents, when they didn't live close by. I never meant for it to embarrass you."

"Well, it does," I said indignantly. "And you shouldn't have posted about me. You didn't even ask my permission!"

At this my parents started to laugh, but then caught themselves. "Well, it's hard to ask for permission from a baby," my dad said. He smiled, but then stopped when he saw the anger in my face.

"So, that just means you didn't have permission!" I retorted.

Just then, I got a text from my friend Phillip.

Phillip 11:05 AM

I always knew you had a good head on your shoulders. I mean, you really know how to use your head! You're a head above the rest!

I immediately turned red with anger.

Eric 11:06 AM

Not happy. Me = fool

Phillip 11:07 AM

Nah, it's funny. You're a 🌟 ! Everyone's sharing it.

A star? That's not how I saw it.

Eric 11:08 AM

How would you like to look like a fool on the Internet? And who is everyone??

Ignoring my last question, Phillip sent a picture of the two of us making faces in the camera.

Phillip 11:09 AM

Remember last week at the pool?

I did remember. Phillip and I had gone to the neighbourhood swimming pool together and started taking goofy selfies. We pretended to be bodybuilders.

Eric 11:10 AM

Yeah. So?

Phillip 11:10 AM

Those photos embarrassed me. I didn't think you would care about the video.

I thought I was angry before, but now I was absolutely livid.

Eric 11:11 AM

YOU DID THIS??

Phillip 11:11 AM

It's no big deal!

Eric 11:12 AM

I'm so embarrassed. I can't ever go to school again!

Phillip 11:13 AM

Oh relax. You'll get over it.

I started to text back, but figured there was no point. I threw the phone on the couch and picked up my backpack. I had homework to do.

Chapter 3

Owning it

The next morning, it was back to school for me. I dreaded the entire walk up the hill. I could see kids gathering by the front gate. A few were mimicking bouncing a ball off their heads.

"Great," I mumbled under my breath.

As I approached, the kids started whooping and hollering. "Heads up, Farnsworth!" one kid called out. I kept my eyes focused on the ground and brushed straight past him.

Once inside, I saw Phillip. I was in no mood to talk to him. But he didn't seem to notice – or care.

"Hey," he said. "I've been trying to get ahold of you."

"What?" I said, making it clear I didn't care.

"I'm sorry I upset you. I didn't think you'd get so mad," he said.

"How could you?" I asked, looking up at him.

"Well, those photos you posted last week embarrassed me. I figured you wouldn't care if I posted the video."

"What do you mean, I *embarrassed* you?"

"Those pool pics," he said. "Tasha saw them and has been teasing me all week." Tasha was a girl Phillip had a crush on. "So, you know . . . thanks a lot."

Then I remembered that I had posted some of those selfies of Phillip to my social network. Tasha must have seen them.

"Oh," I said. "I didn't realise . . ."

"But I wasn't trying to make you mad. I was just teasing you back. If you can dish it out . . ."

"Yeah, I should be able to take it," I said.

"At the same time, I didn't mean for you to get teased. I mean, I know what it's like when embarrassing stuff is shared."

"Yeah okay, I'm sorry," I said. "But now what?"

"Well, here's what I learnt," Phillip said. "You can either hide from it or own it."

"How do you mean?" I asked.

"Well . . . ," he said and started to tell me a story.

"Hey, Mr Muscle!" a voice called out. It was Tasha. "Haven't you got some weights to lift?"

Phillip was flustered. He didn't know what to do. Goofy photos of him had been shared all over school.

"Smile," whispered Aron, one of Phillip's other friends. "Or you can run away and never show your face around her again."

Phillip didn't have much of a choice. "Sure do," he said in his deepest voice. "But I keep my weight lifting for after school."

Tasha and her friends giggled. "You've got a long way to go!" she retorted.

"I guess I do. Call me if you need any heavy lifting!" He started laughing, as did his friend and Tasha and her friends.

"Smooth, man, smooth," Aron grinned, as they walked away.

"So, the point is, I just owned it," Phillip told me. "At first I wanted to run away, but then I realised I could never outrun it. And besides, the photos were funny."

"I don't know if I can do that. You have way more self-confidence than I do."

Just then Tasha walked up. "Hi, Phillip," she said, smiling. Then she saw me. "Hi, Eric. How's your head?"

I started to get angry, but then I saw Phillip mouth the words "Be cool". I took a breath and thought of the funniest thing I could say. "A bit sore."

Okay, so it wasn't very funny, but Tasha still chuckled.

"I bet," she said with a grin.

Throughout the day, I just tried to roll with the punches. Eventually, I came up with a pretty good response. "Coach always said to use my head. He just wasn't specific enough." That got a few laughs.

When school ended, I headed home feeling like I had weathered the storm. That's when Dinky, one of the school's meanest kids, came running up to me.

"Hey, I saw that video," he said. I was about to use my "Coach said" line when Dinky went in for the kill. "Who knew that little butt-rash baby could grow up to be such a big butt-rash baby?"

Everything I had done during the day to calm myself and tell myself that everything was fine went away. I was angry all over again.

Chapter 4

Stop sharing!

"That blog has to come down," I shouted when I walked into the house. Mum was not pleased.

"That is not how you speak in this house," she said. "When you can calm yourself to have a conversation, let me know."

I took a few deep breaths – in through the nose, out through the mouth – and felt my heart rate drop.

"Okay," I said. "Could we please talk about the baby photos and that blog?"

"Of course," my mum said. "Tell me what's going on."

I explained how Dinky had been teasing me about it and that it was embarrassing. I was already dealing with the basketball video and managed to get through the day. But the blog was just too much. At least the basketball game happened in public. My baby butt-rash was a private thing.

"To be honest," said Mum, "I never thought about it that way. It just seemed like it was part of my life as a mother back then. I should have recognised it might be embarrassing for you as you got older. Let's see if I can delete it."

Mum pulled up her blog. She had written a lot about me and my brother when we were little. Most of the posts were about the challenges of parenting – although I don't see what's so hard about it. You just tell your kids what to do and then make them go to their room if they don't do it.

"Okay, here's this one on the rash," she said. "Want me to delete it?"

I nodded. She clicked the delete button.

"Now, about the photos and videos," she said. "I think I can bulk delete them this way." She moved the cursor and selected various images.

Just as she was about to hit "delete", I spoke up. "I've been thinking," I said. "I guess the photos are okay."

My mum looked surprised.

"It's just, I didn't know any of this was here," I said. "I didn't know people could see that stuff, and when I found out, I kind of freaked."

"I know, honey," my mum said. "You felt like your privacy was invaded. That's understandable."

"Yeah," I said. "But when I talked to Phillip, he said sharing photos was no big deal. He thinks it's funny."

"That doesn't mean you have to feel the same way," my mum said. "Everybody has their own ideas about what should be private. If you want them gone, then let's delete those photos."

"Really . . . it's okay, Mum. They are cute photos. You can leave them up."

"What about this one of you drooling?"

"Yeah, that's okay, too. Everybody was a baby once." I paused for a moment. "But I'm glad we deleted the butt-rash blog post. That was a little too much."

Back in my room, I looked up the basketball video again. It now had 17,812 views. Who were all these people? I knew Phillip was right that I should just embrace what was funny, but I also felt sick knowing there were thousands of people laughing at me. Most didn't even know me!

I started scrolling through the comments. Most were harmless, but a few were hard to read. The meanest comment said I should be banned from basketball courts because I was "an embarrassment to the game".

Chapter 5

Privacy

"Hey, Mum," I said, calling out to her in the backyard. "Do you think we could take down that basketball video?"

"I don't know," my mum said. "I mean, I didn't post it."

"No, I know. But it is just so embarrassing. I wish it wasn't up there."

"Well, let's see what we can do," she answered as she came back inside.

We went to the site that hosted the video and clicked on the site's "help" link; then we looked up "how to remove a video". Eventually, we got to a page titled "Community Guidelines".

"Looks like this is what we need," my mum said.

As we read the page, we learnt that videos can be removed if they show violence, make threats to or harass people, or invade people's privacy.

"That seems like what we're looking for," my mum said.

We clicked on the "privacy" link.

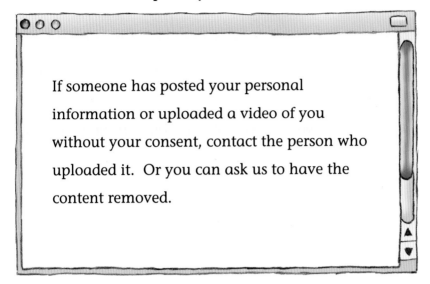

If someone has posted your personal information or uploaded a video of you without your consent, contact the person who uploaded it. Or you can ask us to have the content removed.

"That's it!" I exclaimed.

We wrote a note to the site.

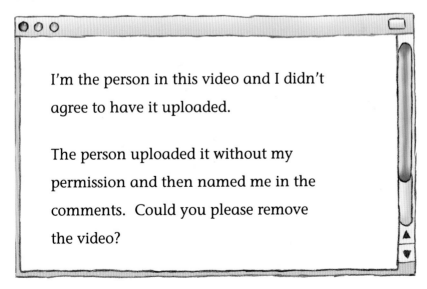

I'm the person in this video and I didn't agree to have it uploaded.

The person uploaded it without my permission and then named me in the comments. Could you please remove the video?

Then I clicked the "submit" button.

I felt better, but I didn't know if the video would be removed. A few hours later, I received an email from the site. It said:

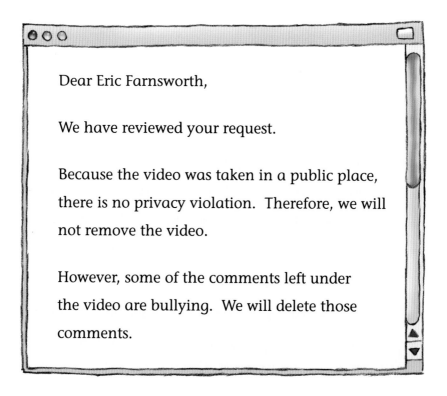

Dear Eric Farnsworth,

We have reviewed your request.

Because the video was taken in a public place, there is no privacy violation. Therefore, we will not remove the video.

However, some of the comments left under the video are bullying. We will delete those comments.

It wasn't the response I hoped for, but I understood. And I appreciated the site removing the mean comments.

As I read over the email, I decided I had one more thing I needed to do.

I grabbed my basketball and headed outside. I needed to work on my jump shot.

A note from the author

When I was young and I left home to go to university, I was excited because it meant I could start a new identity. All of the silly or embarrassing things I did in high school or before weren't going to follow me to university. I had a blank slate.

That's not as true for kids today. So much stuff is on social media and it follows you forever. I worry about kids and social media because they won't get that same opportunity. It's normal to do embarrassing things, but you should be able to escape your past.

Then again, maybe if we all saw each other make more mistakes, we'd be more forgiving and less judgemental. Maybe we'd realise nobody is perfect. What do you think? Are we better off seeing each other's flaws, or should we be able to wipe embarrassing moments from the Internet?